SURVIVING WORK

Using Godly Wisdom to Overcome Work Challenges

KERRY-ANN BARRETT

DEDICATION

To mom and dad.

CONTENTS

PREFACE

Ever since man's fall in the garden, we have been faced with the inevitable truth of labour. "And unto Adam he said, "In the sweat of thy face shalt thou eat bread, till thou return unto the ground; for out of it wast thou taken: for dust thou art, and unto dust shalt thou return." (Genesis 3:17-19). This sentence was passed on to man in general. While some of us enjoy our jobs, there are many individuals who dread the first day of the work week and celebrate the end of the same. A reason for this is the fact that many are constantly persecuted and endure serious struggles in the work environment.

There is however, hope for all and it is centered on a relationship with Christ. There is no need to be burdened down by your employment or anything else for that matter. The word of God says, "Take my yoke upon you, and learn of me; for I am meek and lowly in heart: and ye shall find rest unto your souls. For my yoke is easy, and my burden is light." (Matthew11:29-30). We do this by ensuring our connection and relationship with God stays intact and is not severed by the subtle but deadly attacks of the enemy.

In this devotional, the main character of focus is Daniel and how his relationship with God caused him to excel during his time of work persecution. It depicts how Daniel, a prince of Judah who would have been a privileged child, dealt with the situation he was placed in against his will. He became a servant in the palace of the King of Babylon. We sometimes go through similar situations. However, it is necessary for us to understand that in all of this, God will bless us wherever life sends us, if we trust in Him. It maybe that similar to Daniel, you find yourself in a situation outside of your doing; it was forced on you. This devotional wants to take you to that place, where you can, through God, make the best of your circumstances and watch Him work it out for you. I pray you will be blessed.

DAY 1:
WHY DO I HAVE TO WORK HERE?

<u>Reading:</u> 2 Kings 20: 14-18, Daniel 1: 1-4

<u>Thought:</u> We will fall in different situations, but despite our challenges, we have a God that wants to be our companion through it all.

It is a horrible feeling to be sitting at home on the eve of the start of the work week and instead of being grateful for the fact that you have employment in terrible economic times, you dread the very thought of going to work the next day. I have personally reached this point. After running into roadblocks after roadblocks at work, I just felt backed into a corner and I just could not take it anymore. After making many suggestions that were ignored only to be asked to implement them when other things failed, I got very discouraged. Too many problems created that could have been avoided only to be stuck with fixing them. I thought, "Let them deal with it. They created it, let them fix it." I just wanted to fold my hands. Then the Lord ministered to me through Daniel's story.

> *"In the third year of the reign of Jehoiakim king of Judah came Nebuchadnezzar king of Babylon unto Jerusalem, and besieged it. And*

the Lord gave Jehoiakim king of Judah into his hand, with part of the vessels of the house of God: which he carried into the land of Shinar to the house of his god; and he brought the vessels into the treasure house of his god. And the king spake unto Ashpenaz the master of his eunuchs, that he should bring certain of the children of Israel, and of the king's seed, and of the princes; Children in whom was no blemish, but well favoured, and skilful in all wisdom, and cunning in knowledge, and understanding science, and such as had ability in them to stand in the king's palace, and whom they might teach the learning and the tongue of the Chaldeans" (Daniel 1:1-4). Be sure to read 2 Kings 20:14-18 for further context.

Daniel and his friends were caught in this dragnet. They were dealt a bad hand. Can you imagine, a young man of royal lineage dragged away to serve another king? He was probably looking forward to being "fruitful and multiplying" like his forefathers, only to find out he'll be castrated into a eunuch. For many young men today, that would be the most horrifying thing. Daniel's manhood was taken away. He had to forget about having children. This had to be a painful experience both physically and emotionally. If this wasn't enough, he was then put to serve a heathen king that practiced idolatry. He had a sticky situation to deal with.

But what did Daniel do? Did he fold his hand and say I'm done? Did he turn his back on his God for allowing this? Did he try to sabotage his new master? NO! He served as unto God. Daniel didn't allow the fate that he was dealt to change his character. We have to do the same despite the pressures affecting our physical and emotional wellbeing. A popular part of Jamaican culture is the sorrel drink during the Christmas season. In making the drink, you'll have to boil ginger and pour that hot ginger water over freshly picked sorrel in a container. This is usually left to sit overnight. Once the container is reopened the water becomes a reddish crimson taking on the colour characteristics of the sorrel. We have to ensure that when we are placed in adverse situations (hot water), we display our true godly character and infuse the situation with a testimony of our God.

To extract the fragrance in making perfume, a crushing process takes place. It is no different with us. When we are persecuted and we behave in a godly manner, a sweet-smelling fragrance goes up to the Lord. So even though you might find yourself in a desperate situation that may or may not be any fault of yours, know that it is not the end of the road. Just serve and trust your God. We will fall in different situations, but despite our challenges, we serve a God who wants to be our companion through it all. I have found that when I focused more on the things about my job that I delight in, I'm better able to overcome my negative circumstances.

Tip of the Day: Focus on those things about your job that you appreciate. Write them down.

DAY 2:
KNOW AND BE WHO GOD SAYS YOU ARE

Reading: Daniel 1: 3-21

Focus Thought: We are not defiled by what we are called but more so what we do

Years ago, I accepted a job as an office manager. This office was in disarray, and things were just very poorly organized. I was tasked with managing a group of people who had all gelled together and felt that one of them should have been promoted to my new position. They gave me hell in the two weeks I was there. They would call me names and say cruel things behind my back. I was much younger with little to no tolerance, so I resigned from the position. I realized that patience and longsuffering did not come overnight. I've also learnt that even if I run away from it, if it's something that God wants to use to mould me, I'm going to end up right where God intended. So now instead of running, I seek the Lord through prayer, to enquire what he wills me to do. That way, I don't get stuck going around the same mountain.

After a few years of moving on from that job, one of the young ladies came to work in another organization where she would be reporting to me. Though I knew all she had said and done prior, I welcomed her.

My actions may have seemed foolish, but I've learnt that it's not good to render evil for evil. They are free to call me what they want, but I don't have to take on the character of those names.

Daniel, Hananiah, Mishael, and Azariah were taken to Babylon and given new names. "Unto Daniel the name of Belteshazzar; and to Hananiah, of Shadrach; and to Mishael, of Meshach; and to Azariah, of Abednego" (Daniel 1:7). When we enter the work realm, we are many times branded with names God did not give us; lazy, unproductive, thief, delinquent, unpunctual, ineffective, inefficient, and the list goes on. The same fate was allotted to the Children of Judah. They were given Babylonian names, a first step in erasing their identities. These names did not identify them with the God they knew. However, despite being called by such unfitting names, they kept the character of who they were. They did not take on the nature associated with those names.

These four were made into eunuchs and were being prepared to serve the Babylonian king. A part of that process included eating whatever the king provided. Daniel and his friends took a position that they would not defile themselves by eating the king's meat and drinking his wine. They instead asked for pulse and water. After ten days, they were fairer and fatter than all the children who ate the king's meat (Daniel 1:11-17). When they were brought before king Nebuchadnezzar there were none like these four. "And in all matters of wisdom and understanding, that the king enquired of them, he found them ten times better than all the magicians and astrologers that were in all his realm" (Dan. 1:20).

Maybe you have a supervisor that is highly critical of you, seizing every opportunity to get you fired, or often finding fault with your work when there is none; continue being a child of God. Do your best and appreciate where you are now. Don't become a complainer. Even if a supervisor or another co-worker complains about the job, do not be a partaker. God is not fond of us murmuring or complaining. Philippians 2:14 states, "Do all things without murmurings and disputing." "Neither murmur ye, as some of them also murmured, and were destroyed of the destroyer" (1 Corinthians 10:10). "But ye, beloved, building up yourselves on your most holy faith, praying in the Holy Ghost, Keep yourselves in the love of God, looking for the mercy of our Lord Jesus Christ unto eternal life" (Jude 1:20-21)

Look to God for deliverance in trying times. We cannot give our enemy any ammunition. In this case, complaining is giving the devil bullets to shoot at us. Daniel decided not to defile himself, and we have to do the same. Similar to how Daniel refused to partake of the king's meat because it would defile him, we have to refuse taking on attributes not of God. We should not allow bitterness to stop us from doing what we know is right. We should show up early, be effective, efficient, honest and trustworthy. These are traits of the people of God and this is the way we should be. Even if everyone else on the job practices dishonesty, we have to be different.

The scripture above does not say why the king's meat would defile Daniel, but Hebrew culture prohibits the consumption of certain types of meat or anything sacrificed unto idols. This is considered an abomination. Daniel and his companions clung to this even in captivity and God honoured them with skill, wisdom, knowledge and understanding. They also found favour with the king. At the end of their allotted time of eating pulse and drinking water, their appearance was better than all the others. They proved that God was able to keep them even in this. Let me ask this one thing of you. For ten days, make a constant decision to not complain and instead pray about the matters that affect you. I am confident you will prove that God honours His words.

Giving up meat for pulse may seem like a foolish choice, especially in captivity, but if it honours God, then it's worth it!

You might be ridiculed for doing the right thing but know that God will honour you. He will bless you, causing you to have favour with the very people who want to defile you. God will make you exceptional. Even if you are not liked, it will be clear that your employer cannot do without you. You may lose possessions, people and positions but it is what we do for Christ that will last.

Tip of the Day: Do not complain, even if you are accustomed to doing it all the time.

DAY 3:
GLORIFY HIM WITH THE GIFTS HE GIVES

<u>Reading</u>: Daniel 2:1-23

<u>Thought:</u> Sometimes impossibilities come so those around you may also know the God you serve.

Faced with a dire situation imposed by the external organisation that governed our firm, lack of management support, staff members who dodged accountability and clients who were looking to hear good news as this had serious implications for their livelihoods, I was stressed to say the least. I just felt like giving up. It just seemed impossible. Without a team approach it just didn't make sense. But how could I forget the most valuable player on my team? The one who hired me? The one who specializes in things thought impossible? When I yielded to Him, the Lord came through in a remarkable way that resulted in my promotion.

The All-Knowing God Reveals Secrets to His Servants

In his second year of reign, the king had a dream but could not remember what it was about. He called for the magicians and astrologers, but they were unable to help him. He expected them to interpret a dream he himself could not recall. Their reply was: "There is not a man upon the earth that can shew the king's matter: therefore there is no king, lord, nor ruler, that asked such things at any magician, or astrologer, or Chaldean" (Daniel 2:10).

The king became angry as the dream had troubled his spirit causing him to lose sleep. He decided to kill all the magicians, astrologers and Chaldeans. This group included Daniel and his friends. Daniel asked the king for some time so that he could tell him the interpretation to the dream. He then got together with his three friends. These young men sought the Lord to reveal the secret unto them and the Lord did. Daniel worshiped the Lord: "O thou God of my fathers, who hast given me wisdom and might, and hast made known unto me now what we desired of thee: for thou hast now made known unto us the king's matter" (Dan. 2:23).

Sometimes when our back is against the wall the first solution seems to be, giving up. When the magicians heard the king's request, they concluded that it was impossible, and they were all sentenced to death. Daniel, however, knew better. He recognised that the only way he would escape this situation, was through God. If we maintain our Godly integrity in carrying out our work responsibilities, He will make ways for us through the impossibilities. This reminded me of another testimony, how I was miraculously promoted to a position I was not qualified for, and even then, God gave me the wisdom to fulfil my duties efficiently. In Daniel's story, none of the other wise men were able to interpret the dream, but we see how the Lord gave the answer after Daniel and his friends sought Him.

What impossible situation are you facing at work? A deadline? The possibility of redundancy? A hard task master? Threats? If you are a child of God, living God's way, seek Him and He will give you an answer. This answer many times leads to a promotion. Keep in mind that when you are elevated, that it is not of your own doing but by the hand of God. Glorify Him! That is what Daniel did (Daniel 2:20-23).

Sometimes impossibilities come so those around you may also know the God you serve.

Daniel received the answer from God and his life and that of his friends were spared. God can save you too, regardless of your adversity. If you are living God's way, be assured it will work for your good. God's will must be done while you are at the same time, fulfilling your purpose.

Tip of the Day: Compliment the work of others, especially those who dislike you.

DAY 4:
PROMOTION COMES FROM OBEDIENCE TO GOD

Reading: Daniel 2:23-29

Focus Thought: "For promotion cometh neither from the east, nor from the west, nor from the south. But God is Judge: he putteh down one, and setteth up another" (Psalms 75:6-7).

Not only have I dealt with subordinates not wanting me at the job but had the same issue with a supervisor. In one situation, a supervisor would try every means to put down my work. It got to a point where I said this is not worth it—as it was just too much torment. Then a higher position became vacant at the company that she applied for and was promoted. I was in peace! I no longer reported to her. She then performed poorly in that role and was asked to leave. When she supervised me, she often passed off my work as her's. She did not have this luxury after being promoted. One year later, I was promoted to her initial position and then to the one she moved to. I never applied for any of these positions.

Mystery Solved

Daniel was brought before the king in haste to interpret his dream.

> *"The king answered and said to Daniel, whose name was*

Belteshazzar, Art thou able to make known unto me the dream which I have seen, and the interpretation thereof? Daniel answered in the presence of the king, and said, The secret which the king hath demanded cannot the wise men, the astrologers, the magicians, the soothsayers, shew unto the king; But there is a God in heaven that revealeth secrets, and maketh known to the king Nebuchadnezzar what shall be in the latter days."

Daniel told the king the dream and the interpretation thereof. What the king did next was unexpected. He declared Daniel's God, a "God of gods and a Lord of kings, and a revealer of secrets, seeing thou couldest reveal this secret." He then blessed and promoted Daniel, making him ruler over the province of Babylon and Chief of the governors that were over the affairs of the wise men of Babylon. Daniel requested the King to promote his three friends while he sat at the gate.

Daniel was promoted because he with God's help did what the other wise men admitted could not be done. He was not selfish with it. He remembered his friends that helped him to pray and asked for them to be promoted too. We are blessed to bless others. We serve a God of love, not one of selfishness. Have you ever experienced an ant invasion, one that within minutes of leaving food unattended it becomes hijacked? I don't know how they do it, but they have some sort of texting network where when one ant finds some food, they text the others for backup; they share. This is unlike the individualism that is promoted today. I found the gold so I'll keep it for myself, even if it means I will not get to cash it in because it's too heavy a load for me alone to carry. When God blesses us, we must understand that we cannot afford to be proud or high-minded; looking down on others. Don't forget the individuals that supported you. Daniel remembered his friends that prayed with him.

When you are promoted, please don't forget God. I have seen situations where God promoted people, but they became so inflated with pride that they started to look down on the very things of God. All because they are now where they have always wanted to be in life. Be careful not to follow this example. The same God who promotes, will also demote. Be humble in executing your daily functions whether your position is great or small.

We must also remain faithful to the things of God. Whatever you did before, continue; don't stop tithing because the amount seems too great to give. Continue to pray and read God's holy word. Continue to live right. Continue!

Tip of the day: Ensure that you fulfil all duties assigned to you and more.

DAY 5:
DON'T BOW

Reading: Daniel 3:1-19

Thought: Whatever the sentence of standing up for God is, take it! God is not a debtor to any man.

Integrity is important. I've had a situation where I was given a pre-prepared document to sign and submit to an external organization. Upon my investigation the document was fraudulent. I didn't sign it and was willing to lose my job over it. Sure enough, I became an enemy to some members of the team, but I stood my ground as a Christian. The Lord then did something I didn't see coming. He removed all those individuals, even the ones more senior than I was.

We Won't Bow!

Perhaps it was influenced by the dream he had, but Nebuchadnezzar built an image then gathered all his officers to be present at its dedication. He then commanded that, "at what time ye hear the sound of the cornet, flute, harp, sackbut, psaltery, dulcimer, and all kinds of musick, ye fall down and worship the golden image that Nebuchadnezzar the king hath set up: And whoso falleth not down and worshippeth shall the same hour be cast into the midst of a burning fiery furnace" (Daniel 3: 5-6).

Certain men at the gathering saw that Shadrach, Meshach and Abednego were not bowing to the image and reported it to the king. He was fuming and commanded his guards to bring these three to him.

> *"Nebuchadnezzar spake and said unto them, Is it true, O Shadrach, Meshach, and Abednego, do not ye serve my gods, nor worship the golden image which I have set up? Now if ye be ready that at what time ye hear the sound of the cornet, flute, harp, sackbut, psaltery, and dulcimer, and all kinds of musick, ye fall down and worship the image which I*

have made; well: but if ye worship not, ye shall be cast the same hour into the midst of a burning fiery furnace; and who is that God that shall deliver you out of my hands?"

(Daniel 3: 14-15)

The young men, firm in their faith, were not fazed by the threats of the king. Their response was: "O Nebuchadnezzar, we are not careful to answer thee in this matter. If it be so, our God whom we serve is able to deliver us from the burning fiery furnace, and he will deliver us out of thine hand, O king. But if not, be it known unto thee, O king, that we will not serve thy gods, nor worship the golden image which thou hast set up" (Daniel 3: 16-18). The king became enraged and commanded the furnace to be heated seven times more.

Ever had an encounter at work where you had to do something wrong or else? Maybe it was backdating a document, fraudulently recording figures, or signing off on inferior products? Things of that sort. People are not happy when you go against their will. Some situations even resort to "either you get with the program or leave." Well, these Hebrew boys were faced with a similar predicament. As far as they were concerned, there is but one God and they were commanded to only worship Him. It would be a sin for them to bow before Nebuchadnezzar's golden image and as such they were willing to die for that cause.

A Christian's confidence has to be grounded in the King of kings. If He brings you to a position, He can keep you there. Be careful not to get caught up in believing that you have arrived and hence must go with the flow to maintain status. You should honour God first in all. Even though you get to keep your job and may even receive some extra cash, just say no! If you lose your job, it may be that God has a better one lined up for you. "Yet if any man suffer as a Christian, let him not be ashamed; but let him glorify God on this behalf" (1 Peter 4:16). Whatever the sentence of standing up for God is, take it! God is not a debtor to any. "For whosoever will save his life shall lose it; but whosoever shall lose his life for my sake and the gospel's, the same shall save it" (Mark 8:35).

There is an old proverb that says, "The higher the monkey climbs, the more he is exposed." As you are elevated, be assured that more eyes will be on you. Many will be for your downfall, especially if you have been granted any favours in the workplace. Elevation should therefore be taken as an opportunity to display a Godly life and not the opposite.

Tip of the Day: Forgive individuals who have wronged you on the job. Ask forgiveness of those you have wronged.

DAY 6:
REMEMBER GOD IS A DELIVERER

Reading: Daniel 3:20-30

Thought: Don't worry about your attackers! You will not always identify them but focus on Jesus!

I watched a colleague of mine go through extreme persecution. He was a stickler for doing things right and was blacklisted by other team members as always delaying processes. He was eventually fired. A few months later, he moved to another country, and was hired in a greater position. Then something crazy happened: one of the persecutors lost their job and another was placed in a serious predicament requiring his help. The same people that plotted against and got him fired then befriended him again. They were seeking his help and hoping he would do the right thing in helping them.

There Is a Fourth Man in the Fire

Nebuchadnezzar ordered the mightiest soldiers to bound Shadrach, Meshach, and Abednego, and throw them into the furnace. The fire was so intense that it devoured the men that cast them in. When the king looked, he was frightened because he saw, not only these three men, but a fourth man walking in the fire without hurt. He made queries of his counsellors and they confirmed that it was three men placed in the furnace.

"He answered and said, Lo, I see four men loose, walking in the midst of the fire, and they have no hurt; and the form of the fourth is like the Son of God. Then Nebuchadnezzar came near to the mouth of the burning fiery furnace, and spake, and said, Shadrach, Meshach, and Abednego, ye servants of the most high God, come forth, and come hither" (Daniel 3:25-26).

They came out unscathed. Everyone on the outside was astonished because the fire had no power over the young men. The king experienced a change of heart and blessed the God of these three men. The king then made a decree.

"That every people, nation, and language, which speak anything amiss against the God of Shadrach, Meshach, and Abednego, shall be cut in pieces, and their houses shall be made a dunghill: because there is no other God that can deliver after this sort. Then the king promoted Shadrach, Meshach, and Abednego, in the province of Babylon" (Daniel 3:29-30).

This is a perfect example of how God comes through when we are faithful to Him and His word. He is a true Deliverer! When He delivers, He does it magnificently and there is no doubt about it. The Hebrew men were thrown into the furnace, but God was with them. The king, who was so furious prior, that he heated the furnace seven times over, was the one who identified the fact that God was with them. The three young men came out of the fire unscathed, while the men, who threw them in, died from the heat.

Have you ever been under attack and the individual whose hand was set to destroy you fell into the same trap? It is no different in the workplace. I have seen it many times. Don't worry about your attackers! You will not always identify them but focus on Jesus! He will cover you!

Remember the story of Haman and Mordecai —how God protected his people (Book of Esther). Often, the same trap that people viciously set becomes the end of their own tyranny. We reap what we sow.

People will know that there is something different about you, which is why their attacks never worked. You can boldly declare that your God is a Protector and

Deliverer. This may even lead others to serving your God, the True Deliverer.

Tip of the Day: Trust the Lord to see you through.

DAY 7:
YOUR GIFT WILL MAKE ROOM FOR YOU

Reading: Daniel 4:1-8

Thought: God will honour the work of your hands

My first full time job paid little to nothing. I was tasked with multiple assignments way outside of my pay grade. I remember at one point looking for another job because all my expenses were not covered. One particular evening as I was getting ready to leave, the director came to me and informed me about the positive feedback he was getting from clients and advised me that I would be getting a wage increase. I didn't know others were seeing, let alone talking about my work, but I gave God the praise because I really needed that increase.

You are probably the newest employee at work, but after a while the quality of your work begins to shine even without you paying attention to it. You serve without eye service and God honours it. Colossians 3:22 warns us, "Servants, obey in all things your masters according to the flesh; not with **eyeservice**, as menpleasers; but in singleness of heart, fearing God." Have you ever been in a work environment where the culture is "let's be a good worker while the boss is present"? This is not expected of the saints of the living God. This type of work attitude will not be honoured by God. However, when you work genuinely and assiduously to achieve your tasks beyond the level of expected service, God will bless your work. When you use those gifts, talents and abilities without being stingy, He will honour the work of your hands. God did not give you these gifts, talents and abilities to bury them until your working conditions become ideal (getting the job that you want), you are expected to use them both physically and spiritually. Let us look at the following example:

The Parable of the Talents (Mt. 25:15-30)

Jesus gave a parable likening the kingdom of God unto a man travelling to another country. He called his three servants and gave them talents. To one he gave five, to the second two and to the third servant, he gave one. "Then he that had received the five talents went and traded with the same, and made them other five talents. And likewise he that had received two, he also gained other two. But he that had received one went and digged in the earth, and hid his lord's money" (Mt. 25:16- 18). Their master returned after a long stay to reckon with them, receiving an additional five talents from the servant he gave the five. The scriptures say that he was pleased and entrusted more to him. From the servant that he gave two talents, he received an additional two talents. This pleased him and so he entrusted more to him also. The third servant was so afraid of trading the single talent and losing it, that he hid it from the world. When his master returned, he went and dug it up and returned it to him. The master, who was angry with him, took the talent away and gave it to the servant that already had ten.

> *"For unto every one that hath shall be given, and he shall have abundance: but from him that hath not shall be taken away even that which he hath. And cast ye the unprofitable servant into outer darkness: there shall be weeping and gnashing of teeth"* (Mt. 25:29-30).

Whatever God has invested in you, He is expecting a return. The slothful servant, who for whatever reason, does not make use of this investment will lose it.

Meanwhile, the servant who works diligently, despite his situation, will be blessed and promoted. Do not allow your situation to dissuade you from using all that God has blessed you with to do your best. This will only limit your promotion. Do it great without murmuring, and watch God work it out for you.

The king looked to Daniel because of the work Daniel did previously. His faith in Daniel was buoyed and he now saw Daniel as the "master of the magicians." Daniel wasn't a magician, but he was connected to a God that made a secret known unto him. Daniel was exalted because he used his gift. What is it that you do well? What is in your hand? How can you apply this at work? Do it and watch God open mighty doors of favour for you.

Tip of the day: Focus on executing your job in excellence and find new ways to improve your service.

DAY 8
BE FEARLESS AND TRUE

Reading: Daniel 4: 19-28

Thought: Do not let the fear of man cause you to go along with something you know is not true. God is an all-seeing eye.

I remember being in a strategic management meeting. The focus of the meeting was to brainstorm various ways to fill the financial deficit being experienced at the time. A suggestion was made to extend a service we offered to fill the gap and everyone accepted. I objected because the plan was to earn four times what we were earning from the service without consideration for an already burdened staff compliment. In addition, the targeted market was already exhausted so we would need to find additional customers from other countries. Majority ruled and my objection was rejected. This new plan caused us to stretch our resources too wide and the overall quality of our service deteriorated. We ended up not giving the service after a while because of low demand. As such, the little we earned before was now lost.

The king had a dream and told Daniel about it. Daniel's thoughts were troubled by this dream as it spoke to the evil that would befall the king. The king told him not to be troubled by the same and with that said,

Daniel told the king the interpretation. Daniel gave the king counsel that if he accepted it, he would see an extension of his peace of mind. "Wherefore, O king, let my counsel be acceptable unto thee, and break off thy sins by righteousness, and thine iniquities by shewing mercy to the poor; if it may be a lengthening of thy tranquillity" (Daniel 4:27).

Do not be afraid to be frank with your employer (respectfully of course). Often, in our desire to be men pleasers, we dress up the truth so that everybody will feel good. The sad thing is this action is not only to the detriment of the company but is also to the death of our very souls. Daniel told the king what his dream meant even though it was bad news. He did not pretty it up. Sometimes decorating the truth only causes confusion. Daniel spoke as he was led in the Spirit and the king accepted his words to be true, because he was proven in the past.

Being proven is often a prerequisite to standing up and telling your superiors that they are doing something wrong, or that you foresee serious problems in the business. There may be times when you know a decision taken by your boss will cost the firm dearly. You may also know of an appropriate solution; respectfully let them know how you feel. Support what you communicate with legitimate reasoning. If it is not accepted, you still would have done your part. The blood is no longer on your shoulders. **Do not let the fear of man cause you to go along with something you know is not right. God is an all-seeing eye.**

Unlike the way we tend to separate or compartmentalize our lives (Christian, worker, mother, father, husband, student, etc), when God looks at us He sees us as a whole, how we operate and what we do. He does not look only at the things we relate to Him, for example, church, worship, the bible etc., but He looks at how we apply His principles to our everyday lives.

Do not lie to yourself and others on the job. Be a true representative of the God you serve. Do not scheme to have others taken out, because the same hole you dig for another might be your very grave.

Tip of the Day: Make suggestions to improve your job.

DAY 9:
DO NOT TAKE BRIBES

Reading: Daniel 5

Thought: Do not accept every gift. Prophets of God cannot be bribed

I remember being in community college and having someone approach me with an offer to pay my tuition and in turn I was to apply for work in an organization, where they expected me to occasionally, fraudulently sign documents. I turned down the offer, but I know of other students at the time who took up similar offers only to end up in prison. One young lady even had her baby in prison.

The Writing is on the Wall

After king Nebuchadnezzar, Belshazzar his son reigned in his stead. He made a feast to thousands of his lords and commanded his servants to bring him the vessels of silver and gold that were taken out of the house of the Lord when Jerusalem was taken. They (the king, his wives, princes and concubines) drank from them. They drank and worshiped their gods. As they were doing this, a hand came and wrote on the wall in a language the king could not understand. The king was troubled and afraid that his loins were loose, and his knees buckled. He then cried out to his servants to bring the astrologers, Chaldeans and soothsayers. He promised them great gifts if they could make known the writing on the wall to him and tell the interpretation of the same. But none of them could and the king was more troubled. Now the queen knew of Daniel from during the time of Nebuchadnezzar's reign and told the king about him. The king sent for Daniel.

When Daniel came before the king, Belshazzar told him his plight and promised Daniel great gifts if he could interpret the writings. Daniel's reply was: "Let thy gifts be to thyself, and give thy rewards to another; yet I will read the writing unto the king, and make known to him the interpretation." Daniel told him that the writing spoke to his father, Nebuchadnezzar's glory and how his pride caused him to lose the kingdom. Daniel also let the king know that he was now following his father's footsteps and the kingdom would be taken away from him. That very night after Daniel interpreted the writing, everything was exactly as he said.

Belshazzar did not heed the lessons his father had to learn about the Almighty God. He too lifted up himself against God. He removed the sacred, dedicated vessels from the house of the Lord and used them for his common purposes. I can imagine the indignation that was stored up in Daniel when he called him. Daniel refused the king's offer for a reward and instead told him about his doom for free.

Have you had superiors or colleagues who made a mockery of your faith? Have they made light of the things you do for God or of your dress code? Have they made fun of the fact that you don't party with them? Have you been taunted for your beliefs, only to be the one everyone runs to when they have a prayer request? Just continue being a child of God. Don't allow the world to cause you to lower your standard. You are a vessel of the living God. You are consecrated. Not to be contaminated with idolatry. Continue praying for those God has set over you in the natural realm. It is God who sets up kings and authorities. If God wanted Daniel to be king that very moment no one could stop Him. We have to put things in the right perspective; we do not have to chase an increase because we know who our God is. **Do not accept every gift. Prophets of God cannot be bribed.**

We need to understand that when we go out to work, we will be interacting with individuals who do not all share our beliefs. Many of them will be dishonest and there will be many attempts for you to join in on the dishonesty. Christian, stand your ground.

Tip of the Day: Share a testimony with a co-worker of how God has helped you on the job.

DAY 10:
CONTINUE IN GOD

Reading: Daniel 6

Thought: Success will come and will at times tempt us to do what God did not intend for us, but the saints of the Living God, must continue to uphold our Godly character.

The Lord brought me into a position where I was given the power and authority to do what I wanted. I didn't have to be subjected to decisions of superiors who did not listen to my input or that of others. I made my own schedule and my input was highly appreciated. Then the tendency to just relax and not do anything started attacking me. God had to remind me that I still had work to do.

Daniel the President

A new king reigned after Belshazzar and he made Daniel a president in his kingdom. Daniel was preferred above all the presidents and princes because an excellent spirit was upon him. Then the attacks came. The other presidents and princes could not find any fault or occasion to destroy him except they found it in the laws of Daniel's God. They concocted a scheme to have the king make a decree that no one should petition any God or man for thirty days, save the king. Anyone that did so would be thrown into the lions' den. This they did knowing very well that Daniel prayed to his God multiple times a day. They beckoned the king, "Now, O king, establish the decree, and sign the writing, that it be not changed, according to the law of the Medes and Persians, which altereth not."

The king signed the writing and Daniel knew about it, yet this did not stop him from praying as was his custom. Similar to what his three friends did under the reign of king Nebuchadnezzar, Daniel stood his ground because he knew who his God was. The other presidents and princes watched Daniel as he prayed and then reported the matter to the king. The king was faced with a dilemma because he did not want to hurt Daniel, but he could not recall the decree. "Now the king spake and said unto Daniel,

Thy God whom thou servest continually, he will deliver thee" (Daniel 6:16). Daniel was tossed in the den and a stone was rolled before the entrance.

The king went back to the palace but could not sleep because he was worried about Daniel. He arose early the next morning and went by the lions' den to see if Daniel was still alive. He was overjoyed to find out what the Lord had done. God had sent an angel to shut the mouths of the lions. Daniel was removed from the den "and the king commanded, and they brought those men which had accused Daniel, and they cast them into the den of lions, them, their children, and their wives; and the lions had the mastery of them, and brake all their bones in pieces or ever they came at the bottom of the den."

He also made a new decree that:

> *"That in every dominion of my kingdom men tremble and fear before the God of Daniel: for he is the living God, and stedfast for ever, and his kingdom that which shall not be destroyed, and his dominion shall be even unto the end. He delivereth and rescueth, and he worketh signs and wonders in heaven and in earth, who hath delivered Daniel from the power of the lions."*

It is easy after tasting success, to settle in our own way, operating by our own will rather than that of God's. After all, we are in charge now and we know that God placed us there, so it must mean that He trusts our judgment. We should be careful not to make such fallacious claims and continually seek the Lord for His will and way. Success will come and will at times tempt us to do what God did not intend for us, but the saints of the Living God, must continue to uphold our Godly character.

In chapter six of the book of Daniel, we are shown how Daniel was promoted to the position of president but most importantly, this did not inflate his ego; Daniel remained humble. Many disliked him because of the favour of God in his life. They set traps to bring him down, but God showed Himself mightily. Likewise, we should do the same. Daniel was indeed a true example of what a Christian ought to be in the workplace. Let us dare to be like him.

Tip of the Day: Ask God for guidance in carrying out work responsibilities.

Conclusion

Though we are many times tempted to ask the question, why do we have to work here? We must be grateful and know that God will see us through whatever comes our way. We serve a God that wants us to despite our situation; continue to be who we are in Christ. It is His desire that we will first be sons of God. In this process, we will have to give up many opportunities for riches, but we have a hope that God will bless us for doing things His way.

We must, in every aspect of our lives, be willing to die for what we know is truth (or true), especially on the job, knowing that God is the true Promoter and Provider. As such, we do not need to worry about those who are against us because God is a Protector. Our gifts will make room for us— no bribes necessary! God is an awesome God. He is truly all we need. This need is not exempt in the workplace. The situation may be hard, but if Daniel did it so can you. All we need is one good example. Be ye empowered to work and carry out your duties God's way. I pray you were blessed.